there had to have been someone

**PONGO TEEN WRITING
from KING COUNTY
JUVENILE DETENTION**

DIRECTOR | SERIES EDITOR
Richard Gold

PROJECT LEADERS
Adrienne Johanson, Martha Linehan

WRITING MENTORS
Eli Hastings, Alex Russell, Alexanne Madison,
Jean Gant, Kara Weiss, Mike Hickey, Ross Cole,
Shira Hasson-Schiff, Vanessa Hooper

PONGO PUBLISHING
Seattle, WA, August 2011

Copyright © 2011 Richard Gold

All rights reserved.

No part of the contents of this book covered by copyright herein may be reproduced or used in any form or by any means – including photocopying, recording, taping, or information retrieval systems – without the written permission of the publisher.

The writers contributing to *There Had to Have Been Someone* retain copyrights on their individual works presented in this volume.

Published in August 2011, by

PONGO PUBLISHING, INC.
PMB 155
2701 California Ave. S.W.
Seattle, WA 98116
www.pongopoetryproject.org
info@pongopoetryproject.org

Publisher: RICHARD GOLD

Designer: CELESTE ERICSSON

Image for cover and pages 1, 25, 45, 65:
Copyright © iStockphoto.com / DNY59, MBPHOTO, Inc

Printed and bound in the United States of America.

Dedicated to all of the Pongo teen writers.

Thanks to the following grantors for their generous support of the Pongo Teen Writing Project and this publication:

CITY OF SEATTLE, OFFICE OF ARTS & CULTURAL AFFAIRS
4CULTURE | KING COUNTY LODGING TAX REVENUE
LUCKY SEVEN FOUNDATION · THE NORCLIFFE FOUNDATION
ONEFAMILY FOUNDATION · THE SEATTLE FOUNDATION
HASBRO CHILDREN'S FUND · ROBERTS FAMILY
MICROSOFT ALUMNI FOUNDATION

The authors in this book are not identified by their real names. Details in the writing have also been changed to protect the privacy and confidentiality of our authors and their families.

CONTENTS

Preface viii

THERE HAD TO HAVE BEEN SOMEONE

CHANTAL	There Had to Have Been 2
DE'SHAWN	Memories 3
GEOFFREY	I Like the Rain More Than the Sun 4
D'ANGELO	Finding Summer Again 5
JADA	What Every Guy Tells Me 6
VICTORIA	When I Look in the Mirror 7
KAYLA	Different Levels 8
CAMERON	Addicted 10
ALEXEI	Worries for You 11
RENATA	Daddy's Girl 12
RODGER	The First and Last Day I Saw My Dad 13
MARINA	When She Says She Loves Me 14
MILES	The Missed and Gone 15
ROSE	Changing My Life Around 16
RICA	You Can't Be Mad Forever 18
JOEY	My Dream 20
DARIA	Goodbye to Juvie! 21
MARLENA	I Wonder 22
IVORY	Doors of Emotion 23

I WANT TO SAY HELLO AGAIN TO THE ICE CREAM MAN

ROSE	Ice Cream Man 26
JULIO	Liquor Makes the World Violent 28
SHAINA	My Dad 29
ERSKINE	Letter to Mom 30

v

ANNETTE	Virginity 32
CHRISTINA	Black 33
LUCAS	The Three Faces of My Monster 34
VALENTIN	Drowning 36
SYDNEY	Sides of Me 38
GABRIELLE	The Love of My Life 40
EUGENIO	Monkey 41
JUAN	My Life 42
CARLOS	What It's Like to Have a Headache 43

QUIET IN THE ROOM, LOUD IN YOUR HEAD

JOSIAH	Quiet in the Room, Loud in Your Head 46
CICELY	I Can Stick Through It 47
MALIK	I Wish Someone Had Told Me 48
QUEEN	Anonymous 49
LAWRENCE	I Wish People Knew 50
FABIO	I Didn't Know the True Meaning of My Life 52
ISAIAH	Compassion? 54
JORGE	To Overcome 55
ISRAEL	The Life Within 56
CRYSTAL	Images 57
CARLISLE	Being in Here 58
ELIJAH	What I'd Change 60
MARTIN	Inauguration 61
THALIA	Don't Forget Me 62
JUSTIN	Today 63

THE FACE OF A CELL

JEREMY	The Face of a Cell	66
CHAPMAN	A Broken Fog	67
JESUS	Gang Pain	68
DAVIS	How Do I Start a New Beginning	69
JERRY	Adult Jail	70
MARIUS	Deep in My Soul	71
JON	Hard to Figure	72
JAIME	Race-Blind	73
TYLER	Every Native	74
PATRICK	All I Wish	76
DONALD	Things That Are Old	77
ANTON	In My Wandering Mind	78
CALEB	Thoughts of a Predicate Felon	79
STEPHEN	Getting Out in 30 Days	80
RUBEN	The River	81
AHMED	My Moment of Birth	82

RICHARD GOLD

Preface

We don't know who we are. We are alienated from the parts of ourselves that hurt and feel unloved. And if, as children, we are overwhelmed by terror and loss, we break down along these fault lines of pain, to become one person with separate lives and segregated feelings, to become disengaged strangers in one mind. We make sense of our dysfunction in the best way we can, by assuming it is our fault. We feel like monsters and unlovable. This is how we suffer from the worst experiences of life.

These words in italics, here and throughout this Preface, are my portrayal of the lives and poetry represented in this Pongo book. The Pongo Teen Writing Project is a 16-year-old volunteer-based nonprofit that mentors personal writing by youth inside sites such as juvenile detention, homeless shelters, and psychiatric hospitals. I am Pongo's founder.

The 63 poems in this volume are samples of 741 poems that were facilitated by Pongo at King County Juvenile Detention in Seattle from fall 2007 to spring 2011. The poems are organized in sections, based on the school year they were created. The authors' names and some details in their poetry have been changed to protect their identities.

To say more about the context and writing, the teens in juvenile detention are awaiting trial or serving sentences for a variety of offenses, from running away and truancy to prostitution, drug dealing, and violent crimes. The consistent theme in the young people's writing is childhood trauma, such as abuse, neglect, and exposure to violence. These traumas have a profound effect on the youth, as shown in their poetry, but the story does not end in hopelessness.

Our segregated feelings are intense, as well as unattributed. Our anger and despair drive us to distraction, including taking drugs and alcohol, including running the streets. We replay past agonies in present days. There is no safe place for us.

We feel alone – that we never belonged at home, that we never belonged outside our own neighborhood. The world is afraid of us, afraid of our pain, which is everyone's unrecognized pain. We feel like monsters and unlovable. We replay our agonies with injured companions. We worry that we have no futures.

The story is difficult, but there is also resilience. Many people who have suffered childhood trauma will struggle as children and teens, and many will recover, often with the help of loving family, caring strangers, and significant others.

And poetry is a miraculous tool for re-assembling the pieces of fragmented consciousness. Through poetry, young people bravely communicate feelings and connect these feelings to experience. At the same time, the poetry of trauma, though terribly sad, is also a basis for pride, a vehicle for openness, a tool for self-maintenance, and a source of great joy.

Among our estranged selves, there is an insightful self with a clear voice that speaks directly from the heart. The voice is unpracticed because no one has listened before. But we use it to heal ourselves. We begin with sadness, which is frightening. We especially desire relationship, but have doubts. We are ready to be purposeful, and wonder if we will succeed.

We are poets. And through creativity we make new connections. Our voice gets stronger as we learn who we are. We are not the awful experiences that have happened to us. We want a better world for everyone. And though we mourn our many losses, we write and dream the future.

Poetry is a tool for healing. Pongo has collected surveys from 500 of its writers, to learn that 100% enjoyed writing (though 33% were new to poetry), 70% wrote about things they don't normally talk about, 99% were proud of their work, and 95% expect to write more in the future.

I hope that readers of this book will go to the Pongo web site, where youth can use Pongo activities to write online, and where teachers and counselors can download Pongo activities and also read about Pongo's teaching approach and techniques. There are hundreds of teen poems for inspiration, as well as my blog on the meaning of the work.

Finally, I would like to acknowledge the many people who make Pongo's work possible. I thank our friends at King County Juvenile Detention, including Pam Jones (director), Karen Kinch (volunteer coordinator), and Lynn Valdez (supervisor). I thank our friends at Seattle Public Schools inside detention, including teachers Neal Baumgardner and Stacy Vida. I thank our friends at King County Library inside detention, including librarian Jill Morrison.

I thank our funders, who are listed on the dedication page. I thank Pongo's talented project leaders and wonderful mentors, who are listed on the title page. And lastly, I thank our authors, who move us, inspire us, and teach us every day.

SCHOOL YEAR **2010-2011**

There Had To Have Been Some One

CHANTAL Age 14

There Had to Have Been

There's no important person in my life.
There just isn't.
Hasn't always been this way.

At some point there had to have been a person
That made me feel
Happy,
As happy as my splat pink hair.

At some point there had to have been a person
That made me feel
Loved,
As loved as a small baby bluebird
In Mama Bluebird's nest.

At some point there had to have been a person
That made me feel
Important,
As important as The President
At her inauguration.

Right now
There's no important person in my life,
But at some point
There had to have been.

DE'SHAWN   Age 16

Memories

I don't have memories.
I forget a lot of things.
I don't remember.
It's easier not to remember
because I do too many bad things.
I don't have memories.
I wish I could remember things
because then I wouldn't feel
this emptiness inside my head.
I don't have good memories.
I wish I had memories
of chillin' with my friends,
but I can't remember anything.
But I know my identity.
That feels good,
to know who I am.
Maybe if I didn't do such bad things,
I could open up to memories.

GEOFFREY Age 13

I Like the Rain More Than the Sun

Wish my wrist was bleeding
To stop my heart from beating
With a blade or a knife
To end this life
Just being in here
And what happens outside of this place
My dad is a druggie
My mom is depressed
And she hasn't stopped crying
Since I've been here
It's a high chance I'll be found guilty
Like my uncle did when he wasn't guilty
The sad thing is
I've felt this way since I was eight
My cousin abused me every day
And my dad can't do anything
He needs drugs to feel happy every day
I like that it's raining
I like the rain more than sun
I like the rain because I can walk in peace
No one will really bother me
Because no one likes the rain
And because of that I feel no more pain

Dedicated to my mom and dad

D'ANGELO Age 17

Finding Summer Again

I cry for freedom.
Freedom is summertime.
It's being myself, being able to cope with others,
Happiness, joy in all life has to offer.
Not being locked up in here.
I cry for summer.

The longer I go without summer,
The crazier I go.
I get upset, unfocused.
Crazy as a black hole that sucks you in and
Traps you with feelings of neglect,
Self-hatred, and despair.

The less I talk,
The more silent I become.
Silent as the night
That fills me with questions, like:
    What am I capable of?
    What are my true intentions?
    What's in my future?
    Is it a good job and raising a family?
    Or is it sorrow, separation, and neglect?

But the biggest question I have is:
    How do I find summer again?
I cry for summer.

JADA Age 15

What Every Guy Tells Me

What every guy tells me is
I love you
I'll never leave you
You're my one and only.
But he has other females
That you never knew about
Until you start messin' with him
And then they come out
Like a jack-in-the-box.
First they wind you up
And then the secrets pop out
And you're surprised.
You don't know what to do.
You walk away.
You keep your jack-in-the-box secrets
And you remember he said
He loved me
He'd never leave me
Or hurt me.
And he turned around and did it.
And this is what every guy tells me.

VICTORIA   Age 16

When I Look in the Mirror

When I look in the mirror,
I see a young lady that's been through hell and back,
colors on the right eye
blind on the left
hatred on the left hand
love on the right.
Sixteen years that I live and already seen
the good and the bad.
But blood on your hands,
you never wanna see that.
Losing a friend or family member is the worst,
especially in front of you.
Just thinking yesterday,
everything was a good day.
But you never know, things can switch up on you
anytime,
any day.

Dedicated to all my loved ones

KAYLA Age 16

Different Levels

There are different levels to
Life being hard.

Some people have homes,
A nice family, maybe not
Brothers and sisters, maybe not
A bed, drawings on the wall, clean floor
Artifacts from dead family members
Or maybe not.

Some people have cardboard
An overstuffed duffle filled with the
Special things you have left
Clothes, books, drawings, things that
Mean something to you
And nothing to the world.

Some people have alleyways
Sharing space with street friends
The only home known to you
Tossing and cold throughout the night because
The blanket can barely cover you both
No choice but to call it home.

Some people have nothing
No friends or family to share a blanket with
No cardboard to lay
No duffle
No things.

I'd never make it in this world alone
Because being alone is truly having nothing.
I've experienced all these levels and
I've always found the light.
I cannot explain all the aspects of life on the street
But hopefully this is a snapshot.

Life on the street can be hard
But your life can still be extraordinary.

CAMERON Age 17

Addicted

I am addicted
I am addicted to crime
In my addiction, my life is filled with sleazy nights
    and grime
In my addiction, I am glad to feel happy at the time

I am addicted
I am addicted to crime
In my addiction, I hate to think about my time
In my addiction, the real me becomes hard to unwind

I am addicted
I am addicted to trouble
In my addiction, betrayal comes in the form of doubles
In my addiction, I struggle to survive on the bubble

I am addicted
I am addicted to trouble
In my addiction, I am hiding my voice behind mumbles
In my addiction, I am in a constant battle with everything
    that is humble

I am addicted

ALEXEI Age 17

Worries for You

My sister,
She just turned thirteen.
Her birthday wasn't great
Because everyone was sad.
A week or two before,
My grandma died.

My sister,
She really likes me, but
I haven't been much of a role model,
Which is a problem.
I don't want her to do drugs,
No smoking, no violence.
I want her to go to college,
Stay focused on important stuff,
Not just the here and now,
But her future.

Sister:
If there was a lesson I want you to learn it's –
It doesn't matter what other people think,
It only matters who you know you are.
Because if you don't know who you are,
You end up losing yourself in others
And becoming something you're not.

Trust me on this.

RENATA   Age 15

Daddy's Girl

Daddy's girl growing up, that was me. I wanted to be like him, quiet and attractive. I was. He was my best friend and mentor, made me who I am today, beyond the cell door. My 10th birthday, my best friend left, and I was broken as s***. F*** this guy, how could he?

And f*** my mom for not being as close to me. She made the next five years hell. Everything I did had to be done myself. Always making me feel bad about my long frizzy hair. I started lifting. Shampoos, make-up, face washes. Obsessed with how I looked. My obsession turned into my dream, my challenge.

By age 13, I was dieting, fasting, running every day. Dying over one zit, dying to be gorgeous. Age 15, got pregnant, got dumped, had a miscarriage. Got addicted to alcohol and everything behind it.

My dad won't talk to a f***-up kid, and my mom's too self-absorbed to praise me for my efforts toward my dream. All I can say is I'm sorry I'm back in juvi. I'm sorry I missed curfew. I'm sorry it's because I was enrolling myself into cosmetology school.

Where's my dad to see me now?

RODGER Age 17

The First and Last Day I Saw My Dad

I remember going on the bus, alone.
When we pulled up to the prison gates,
I was scared.
We got to the visitation office, and I see
This big ol' Native
In a caged room –
My dad.
He told me:
This ain't no place for a real man,
Then asked me to never visit him again.
So I didn't.
I knew what he meant.
When you're locked up
You can't take care of your family,
In a legit way,
Like a real man.

MARINA Age 16

When She Says She Loves Me

As I sit in my cell,
I wonder why my mother
couldn't get me out of juvenile jail.
She is a woman I love,
but also a woman I feel I do not know.
As I think about my past,
I don't remember her there.
She seems to put on an act in front of others,
that's when I truly don't recognize her as my mother.
She has five kids,
but acts as if she only has four.
There are times when I really feel like
I have no one to love me no more.
As I sit in my room and wait to be called for dinner,
I never hear my name.
It doesn't seem to bother her
I'm in so much pain.
But when she says she loves me,
I believe her
'cause she is the woman who gave me birth.

MILES Age 17

The Missed and Gone

The missed and gone:
The homies, family, and etc.

The missed:
Seems like yesterday when my friend was here,
when we all was in the hyph bus,
chilling and kicking it,
laughing and talking,
clowning around.

Gone:
I can't believe life moves so fast.
One day you're here,
the next you're on a R.I.P. tee shirt.
When I was younger,
my older uncles used to tell me life goes on.

The missed:
Is something that's hard to get over,
but eventually
you will move on.

Gone:
Someone who has passed, that there's a bad memory,
but you let go
to go on with life.

ROSE Age 16

Changing My Life Around

My relationship with my family needs to change.
I want to be closer to them.
I want us all to be happy and understand each other.
But for me, with my family now,
I feel outside and unaccepted.

My relationship with education needs to change.
I want knowledge from lots of places.
I want to be influenced by life beyond the streets.
But for me, with my education now,
I feel lost and unaccomplished.

My relationship with my boyfriend needs to change.
I want my voice heard and my problems understood
Without feeling his aggression.
But for me, with my boyfriend now,
I feel like a possession, not a human being.

My relationship with God needs to change.
I want him to take hold of my hand,
Let me know he's there.
I want my heart filled with his spirit, so I know he cares.
But for me, with my God now,
I feel disconnected, like the devil took his place.

How do you fix this?
I don't know.
Struggles and pain will come and go in my life,
But I do know I have the power to change
And move beyond any obstacle.

Dedicated to KF

RICA Age 17

You Can't Be Mad Forever

If I was mad forever,
I'd never get anywhere.
I want to be someone.
You can't be mad forever.

I've been a foster kid
since I was three.
I've had to learn that
I can't run away from my problems.
You can't be mad forever.

My voice isn't heard.
If I could be heard,
I would get the help I need.
You can't be mad forever.

They wonder why I skip school,
why kids steal.
There's always a reason.
You can't be mad forever.

If I didn't know that,
I'd be mad about a lot of stuff.
Maybe it's a good thing
that I am in here.
You can't be mad forever.

When you have no one to lean on
and you fall down a lot,
you've got to pick yourself up.

You can't be mad forever.

JOEY   Age 17

My Dream

My most favorite entrée is pork chops. I wash 'em off in water. I season 'em with pepper and salt, garlic powder and onions, red hot hot sauce. After that I sprinkle a little water and dip 'em in flour.

It's a feeling of enjoyment I get when people taste my food. Makes me feel good inside to know that they enjoy something I made.

Next is mac and cheese. Get a pot filled half with water, boil the water, cook the noodles; and when the noodles stick to the wall, they're done. Then I put 'em all in another pot. I get two cheeses – American and cheddar. I slice and dice the cheese into the pan and put the pan in the water. When it comes out, you got cheesy-gooey mac and cheese.

It's a warm and fuzzy feeling I get when I remember the first time I ate mac and cheese. And that's exactly what I want my customers to feel when they come into my restaurant for the first time.

YUM!!!

DARIA   Age 16

Goodbye to Juvie!

Goodbye to Juvie!

Goodbye to all the fake females with their smiles in your face and their talk behind your back.

Goodbye to Juvie!

Goodbye to the grimy food – the spaghetti today, for example, was like burnt charcoal and noodles with no sauce. Goodbye, also, to the famous soggy noodle dish.

Goodbye to Juvie!

Goodbye to someone and all her speeches and lectures about getting on track.

Goodbye to Juvie!

Goodbye to Juvie love, to all the whispers and sneakiness, the feeling of longing, the secret kisses in the library.

Goodbye to Juvie!

Goodbye to Pongo, to the good-looking volunteers and the rough, addictive, secretive, heartfelt poetry that they've yanked out of me!

MARLENA Age 15

I Wonder

I wonder what a happy family feels like.
I wonder if my friends actually care.
I wonder what it's like to be responsible.
I wonder what my little brother is doing.
I wonder if there really is a God.
I wonder what God would say to me
    if he watched over me like people say he does.
I wonder if my little brother is going to school.
I wonder if his parents are still dope addicts.
I wonder what my mom thinks of me.
I wonder if my mom knew everything that went on
    when I was little.
I wonder why my mom acted like she didn't know.
I wonder if in the future I'll still be with my boyfriend.
I wonder why people have addictions.
I wonder if my dad really cared when I was little.
I wonder if my dad is sober.
I wonder if he has a job.
I wonder what my dad thinks about.
I wonder if I will ever have a happy family.
I wonder if I will sit down and eat dinner and play games
    with my family.

Dedicated to my mom

IVORY Age 15

Doors of Emotion

I'm opening up closed doors
Behind one door I find sadness
It's blue, it's boring, it's lonely, it makes you cry

Behind another door
You see happy people enjoying things they like
You hate them because they're happy, and you're not
So you slam the door and move to the next one

The next door is terrifying
You see guns and drugs and people dying
It's a dangerous door to walk through

There's a door in my heart
It's so full that when you open it
Everything comes tumbling down
All the frustrations, the joys, the hate, the love

Somewhere in there is the perfect life
A perfect me

SCHOOL YEAR **2009-2010**

I Want To Say Hello Again To The Ice Cream Man

ROSE Age 16

Ice Cream Man

I just thought you should know
that sometimes I'm afraid of you.
I don't mind you rep'ing the gangs,
but sometimes when I look into your eyes,
I see violence against me,
I see violence against your grandma,
and it hurts me inside.

I just thought you should know,
I want to work in here someday,
helping kids that went through what I went through,
help them understand why I ran away from home,
because my parents beat me,
because the stress in my life
made me do something stupid.
I was the girl who stopped going to school,
I was the girl who stopped listening to her parents,
who started drinking and smoking.

I just thought you should know
that one side of me wants to be with you
and one side of me does not,
and the side that does not is confused,
feels like a lost sheep.

I just thought you should know,
I see myself with a happy family
in a park, Oakland, CA, eating barbecued lamb
next to the swimming pool while dads play tennis
and moms talk and serve food
and all the Tongan people speak to the ice cream man.

I just thought you should know,
I'm tired of seeing what people do on the streets,
and I'm tired of being a part of it.

I just thought you should know,
I want to say hello again to the ice cream man.

———

Dedicated to Z

JULIO Age 16

Liquor Makes the World Violent

It's in my blood to be a drunk.
I can only think of one person
who don't drink in my family,
my brother, who's a Jesus freak.

Things that are bad about drinking:
    Kills muscle
    Kills your brain
    Kills your liver (my mom's liver is really bad from drinking)
    Violence

I don't like that it makes my family violent.
And it makes me violent, too,
'cause I've got anger inside.

Out on the street corner,
I don't even remember the night
I was out beefin' with another gang,
got jumped,
woke up in my bed
all bloody.
I don't even remember the night.

I think liquor makes the world violent.

Dedicated to my mom and family

SHAINA Age 15

My Dad

My dad is the coolest dad,
But he's not the best dad.
Once I smoked meth with him.
I know that's really bad.
He was never really like a dad,
But he always bought me stuff,
Gave me money –
He said to make up for lost time.

He is the coolest dad,
He lets me and my friends hang out at his house,
But he smoked meth with all my friends
And my boyfriend,
And I didn't even know.
He never tells my secrets to anyone, not even my mom.
But he acts like he is my age,
Not like an adult.
I used to run away a lot,
And I could hide out with him.
He would always tell me I should make different choices
Than him,
But he will support me no matter what.

ERSKINE Age 15

Letter to Mom

I haven't seen you in seven months.
You are addicted to drugs.
Last time we had a house, I was eight.
But I want to apologize to you because I'm in juvie.
My older brother went to jail.
You're in jail now.
So this is my letter to you in jail, from juvie.

The first thing I want you to know is
That I'm facing two years, and that's a long time.
I made a mistake.
We all make mistakes.
Mom, you know something about that.
You would steal to support your habit.
But I appreciate you for making sure we had
Food and clothes.
I want to thank you for not doing drugs
In front of me.

Another thing I want you to know is
That I'll be staying at Grandma's when I'm out,
And going to school.
I'm not failing.
I'm disappointed that I'm in juvie.
I want to be free and in school.
You went to college for three years.
Thank you for showing me that school is important.

The last thing I want you to know is
That I love you.
And our family is gonna be okay.
M. is talkative and observes a lot.
He's really enjoying preschool.
T. is a cheerleader now.
She's getting A's in school and growing up fast.
She's still got her attitude,
But is learning to control it.
I think you would be proud.

As for me, I play basketball.
I enjoy drawing and writing.
I'm trying to quit drinking.
Mom, you know something about that.
I appreciate how you keep up with us,
Letting us know you're okay.
We know you're trying, and
We continue to pray for you.

Dedicated to Mom

ANNETTE Age 16

Virginity

I feel like I want to run away
but I've got no place to hide

I feel empty inside
no emotions except anger and sadness

I feel lonely

I feel like I want to speak
but I don't have a voice

I feel like I'm trapped in a cage
and I don't know where I put the key

This is the pain of something special
getting taken away
but it wasn't my choice

CHRISTINA Age 17

Black

The One Pleasure pulses through my veins,
I sigh in relief and look up at my friends:
The ones I care for, the ones I love,
Slowly going mad as they lose everything to the black –
Money, home, cars, life,
Wasting away as they wait and search for that "last hit,"
Letting go of everything around them,
Replacing it with a tiny space full of cockroaches
They call "home."

"Please," I plead, "When will you quit?"

We all scream this inside,
But all we care about is the black –
Nurturing it, feeding it.
They all are scared of losing it, getting sick,
So the black pulls them back further
Into the single-mind of addiction.

Losing everything is not worth this.
Crying and screaming every night is not worth this.
Giving up friends and family is not worth this.
Watching close ones choose death is not worth this.

So I pray that you never make this mistake,
That you never give way –
> for it will swallow you
> for it will become you

LUCAS Age 15

The Three Faces of My Monster

1.
I feel like a monkey in a cage with so much rage
& fear
the fear my mom is dying
the fear I am out of control
like a monster is living inside me
he sees blood & death every time he opens his eyes
everybody runs & hides
he has nothing but anger accelerating through his body
like getting hit with electricity
still locked up, I woke up & looked in the mirror
I changed, & not in a good way
I always look drugged up
nobody trusts me
because the monster hurts people
doesn't feel the pain & sadness
laughs like it's a joke

2.
now, I am out of jail with freedom
but I am scared to lose it
now I am walking down the street in the dark
by myself
anger built up like I'm going to kill somebody

I'm scared of the monster in me
the monster takes away my freedom like a basketball
every time
the next minute I'm running
because I'm getting shot at
the next minute I get shot in the head

3.
I am finally free of the monster
happy knowing I ain't going to get hurt
or hurt anybody else
it's like I'm a man on top of the world
with my grandpa
I imagine how my life would be
if I didn't have the monster in me
now, I am finally free
I can look down on my family
all the people I've hurt
& say goodbye

VALENTIN Age 17

Drowning

We have had three consecutive years,
Same day each year,
Where someone in my family drowns.

First year, my cousin's grandma,
She was drinking water.
Her husband found her.

Second year, my cousin on his fifteenth birthday,
He fell off a waterfall.
They found his body three days later.

Third year, my brother drowned
In our big, backyard swimming pool.
My sister stepped on him, in the pool.
The chlorine water was foggy.
It took the ambulance fifteen minutes to get there.
That was four years ago.

I've been to more than four funerals this year.
All of them, family.
When it happens, I think,
"Here we go again,"
Like it's something that's just gotta happen.
I needed something to forget about it.

I've been smoking crystal meth for the last three years.
It's killing my brain.
I see myself getting slower.
I'm not emotional anymore.
I used to preach as a missionary all over the country.
Now, it's like I'm drowning.

SYDNEY Age 16

Sides of Me

The side that hates me right now is feeling
Irritable, miserable, sad.
I wish I didn't feel this way.
I think about my boyfriend and my
Staffordshire Terrier named Sugar.
Myself is angry with me
For being here.
But I have to cope,
I have to deal.
I should be used to this,
But I'm claustrophobic.
This place makes me
Anxious, nervous.
I threw a bottle of lotion at my wall because
It was the only thing I could break.
But it got me three hours in captive time.

The side that loves me right now is
Hiding,
Doesn't want to be found,
Doesn't want to be talked to.
When something's really funny,
Like old episodes of Tom and Jerry,
That's when I'll smile.
Right now, I don't have much love for myself.
I feel like a failure being here.
I followed everyone's expectations.

They told me I wouldn't be sh**,
I'd be pregnant,
Do drugs,
Drop out.

Even though I'm in jail,
I'm still a kid who
Goes to school, works, and
Listens to parents, even though
My dad's a big pain.
There's this side of me that wants to
Tell them all to
F*** off
And let them know that
Little Sugar and I
See a different path.

I don't want kids until I'm 25 or 30,
When I got
College right,
Career right,
Family material right.
Little Sugar will see,
Even though she won't be little anymore.
We'll be watching Tom and Jerry
with Captain Crunch,
Thinking about all the things
I've done right.

GABRIELLE Age 13

The Love of My Life

We've got a retarded Bordeaux bulldog from the military that sleeps on top of his dog house in the rain. He drools a lot, has paws the size of my palms, knocks down the garbage can to eat, and chewed up my house-arrest ankle monitor.

But he's my baby.

Dedicated to my family and my dog

EUGENIO Age 12

Monkey

When Mom's not home, we go to the park
and pick the plums from the trees.
You like the small ones, but I say
they're not quite ready yet, they're sour,
but you say you like it, you like the sour ones.

The plums aren't there anymore,
all of them fell three weeks before I came here.
We went back to the park, and the plums
were all fallen, all rotten.

It will be summer the next time
we go to get plums from the park.
You'll be six and want to climb the trees
to get them – You also like
bananas, so I call you Monkey.

I miss you.

Dedicated to my sister

JUAN Age 17

My Life

I missed my little sister's birthday, my friend's birthday, my mom's birthday. I missed being there when my friend's mom died. I'm worried about getting sent up to adult jail when I turn 18. I don't want to get deported.

It all started when I cut my house-arrest bracelet. If I could, I would go back to October 2nd and put the scissors back in the drawer – I'd say, "Trust me, man, don't do it."

I heard one of my little cousins was pretending to be on house arrest – He put a metal bracelet on his ankle. If I could, I'd tell him, "You do bad things and get sent to jail, that's how you end up on house arrest."

I want to get out. I want to be with my cousins, go get a job with my dad, get my own apartment, get my GED.

Being here is like a little game, like a little kid thing.

If I do go to jail, it should be for a good reason,
like my dad hitting my mom, and me trying to stop it.

But I always get sent to jail for stupid reasons.

CARLOS Age 16

What It's Like to Have a Headache

When I woke up I had a headache.
It felt like Bulldozing a rock.
I wonder if I think too hard.
I wonder if playing too much tackle football
gives me these excruciating headaches.
I wonder if the headache will ever go away.
I wonder if my Dad is doing OK now,
working hard, watching my L'il sisters.
So much responsibility, Learning to take
care of his loved ones.
I wonder if he will ever change his ways –
Watching us while Drinking,
bringing other Females in while Mom is gone,
or Doing Crank in the bathroom not knowing
who us kids are when he comes out.
As I get older I wonder why
he did these things???
Did he really mean what he says
about how he loves us so much???
As I wake out of my daze there it is,
Another headache.

SCHOOL YEAR **2008-2009**

Quiet in the Room, Loud in Your Head

JOSIAH   Age 16

Quiet in the Room, Loud in Your Head

I wish I was out of here
Because it's too quiet.
It's a loud quietness.
Everything going through your head.
Quiet in the room,
Loud in your head.

I wish I knew God before.
I wouldn't have even hit the dude.
You want to go back with a time machine
And say "Forget about it!"
Quiet in the room,
Loud in your head.

The dude,
He was a lot smaller than me.
I felt I had to do something,
But I really didn't.
The past comes back on you, for real.
I might've forgot, but he didn't.

I regret this happened.
You gotta suffer the consequences.
You may not have a time machine,
But you can still learn from mistakes.
Quiet in the room,
Loud in your head.

CICELY   Age 14

I Can Stick Through It

My life is a living hell.

Like Boys.
They love you, then leave you,
Like a cake with no filling.
But boys aren't the only thing on my mind.

Like Family.
My mom, she's grimy,
But she still cares.
Her love will always be there,
Like a tree with no leaves,
Like a turquoise heart, physically there
But made of stone.

Like Being Homeless.
I don't have nobody.
I'm all on my own, independent,
Like the sun setting
Behind a stormy lake.
Tomorrow has hope.
But tomorrow feels far away.

My life is a living hell,
But I can stick through it.

In memory of my father

MALIK Age 16

I Wish Someone Had Told Me

I wish someone had told me that life was like this,
and I thought I was not going to end up in here,
and it happened.

I wish someone had told me that love was like this,
intimate,
and no lying, cheating, stealing, robbing and all that,
because it does not have to be like this.

I wish someone had told me that friends were like this,
they turn on you and get you in a lot of trouble,
and I wish I would have known that before I put myself
in that predicament.

I wish someone had told me that I was a kid.
I wish that I can start my life over
and do what I have to do
to better myself.

I know these things are true
because it happened all in my life,
and I experienced it, so I think it can be true.

I know these things are true, but still,
I wish someone had told me.

QUEEN   Age 15

Anonymous

I wish I was a better child.
I wish I could take back all the times
    I made my mom cry.
I wish I could take back all the times
    I've hit my little sister.
I wish I had everything I wanted.
I wish I wasn't in Juvenile.
I wish I was still a virgin.
I wish my brother wasn't dead.
I wish my cousin was never born.
I wish that I wasn't a drug addict.
I wish I wasn't an alcoholic.
I wish I went to school when I was younger.
I wish I wasn't in a gang.
I wish there wasn't so many rules
    in this world.

I wish my life was as good as I want it to be.
I wish I could take back all the times
    I made my dad mad at me.
I wish I could take back
    almost killing somebody.
I wish I was still young.
I wish I wouldn't have grown up so fast.
I wish for nothing else to happen to me.
And that's all I wish.

LAWRENCE Age 16

I Wish People Knew

I wish people knew
That I've seen a lot of things...

> I've seen a friend in my face, then later the next day someone come and tell me he died last night.
>
> I've seen a cousin in my face then ten minutes later he's dead. Life flashes in an instant, so live like there's no tomorrow.
>
> I've seen when I was little, on the news, that my little cousin got caught in a fire and died.

That I want to help other people...

> I want to help by becoming a better person
> and be more respectful to people of my surroundings
> and have a fresh start.

That I can make changes...

> I can change by making new friends and start a new era and do more stuff with my little brother than just leaving.

I wish people knew
That I have a lot of feelings…

> Sometimes I feel lost and searching in my dreams for people I lost.
>
> Sometimes I feel mad because I'm following in my dad's footsteps.
>
> Sometimes I feel I'm disappointing my mom and little brother by being detained.

I wish people knew…

> That I am an angry person in the inside, but on the outside I am a nice person.

―

Dedicated to myself

FABIO Age 16

I Didn't Know the True Meaning of My Life

People always telling me that life's a game,
I didn't care what they said, I always smiled the same.
I never took anybody seriously,
I never took myself seriously.
Always testing people,
Always testing myself.

I didn't care whether I lived or died,
Always on the roll like the board and the dice.
Basically I lived my life with no rules,
Getting kicked out of schools.
Didn't care what would come next for myself,
Never felt I belonged,
Like a misplaced book on the shelf.
I never thought about anyone besides myself.

This sort of thing comes from someone
Who grows up in a broken home.
I had never known how it felt to be liked by others,
Only felt what it was like to be hated,
But it's never really bothered me,
Most of the time.

To live life,
Not knowing any values,
Not having any goals,
Not knowing what you want in life,
That comes for someone like me.
I just sit back and drift
Like a boat in the sea.

Dedicated to all the lonely kids out there

ISAIAH Age 16

Compassion?

What is this thing they call compassion?
Is it something that we all have?
Or is it only for the people that have been hurt.
I need to know!
Everyone is telling me I need a little more.
What is compassion? I…
I have been hurt plenty,
I could even say too much.
I say compassion for me is no more.

It was forgiveness.
It was to feel what they feel.
It was to care a little.
How can I have compassion for others…
When there is no compassion for me?

JORGE Age 15

To Overcome

Be like a lion because they're vicious.
I'd like to protect myself from too many feelings.

If I were a lion I'd be strong and
wouldn't have to come to jail.

Be like a rock because you wouldn't have to go through
what I'm going through. I wouldn't have no feelings.

I'm looking at pretty hard time.
I wish my heart was hard like a rock.
I wish I didn't have emotions.

ISRAEL Age 16

The Life Within

My life is not about stars and flowers
but my life is like rocks and dirt.

My life ain't about love fantasies
but it's like killing and shooting.

My life would've been about popularity at school
but now it's just me in my own room.

My life is like tangled ropes without my family
but with them it's untangled, binding us together.

My life is like an empty box that only I know about.
I've tried to fill it with positive thoughts
but the negativity empties it.

CRYSTAL Age 17

Images

There once was a girl that had lost herself in the world's image. She had been used and abused, but wanted more for herself. She felt helpless, like a deep dark pit, one she could not escape.

She had so much potential, but no one to guide, support, or trust her on her long journey, the journey of life.

Until one day she decided to make many changes. At the time, her life was a roller coaster: always twisting, turning, up and down, faster, slower, never knowing the next move till it happened.

Life was complicated like an intricate math problem, algebra, maybe chemistry – all those formulas and stuff some people just plain don't understand.

She felt overwhelmed, like she was in an ocean, endless water all around, and waves constantly crashing over her head, making things hard to do clearly or sometimes at all.

Dedicated to others that are in a struggle such as myself

CARLISLE Age 14

Being in Here

Being in here
It's really cold
You're trying your best to stay good,
but something bad always happens

It makes you sad
because you want to get out
You go to court, and they keep you here,
and that's depressing
Try to call your folks, your family
They don't pick up the phone

Being in here
You toss and turn in your bed
It's hard to go to sleep
You stay up 'til one,
thinking why did I do what I did,
and thinking how I could have changed the situation,
and wondering if your family is thinking about you
as much as you're thinking about them,
or if they've just forgotten

Being in here
It makes you feel...
There are really no words to describe how it feels
It feels like everyone has forgotten
And I ask myself at night,
"Where did everyone go?"

Being in here feels like you're at a shelter,
feels like you're an orphan,
and no one wants to adopt you
You want to cry,
but you don't want to show your emotions
So you sit with a fake smile,
acting like everything is all right
You look into the mirror
and feel like you're going to throw up,
because you know you can do better,
and this is not what your family would want

Being in here is shocking
This is not where I planned to be

Dedicated to my grandmother

ELIJAH Age 17

What I'd Change

Less time in a crowd
More time to myself
Less time tryin' to be grown
More time bein' a son
Less time bein' a class clown
More time respecting my education
Less time taking what I want
More time earning what I get
Less time dissing my family
More time lovin' 'em
Less time thinkin' about the past
More time bettering my future
Less time wastin' money
More time savin'
Less time away in Juvie
More time livin' my life right

Dedicated to CH

MARTIN Age 17

Inauguration

Today Obama stood tall like a tree that's hickory,
Today Barack H. Obama made history.
Today he did what he said he was, and that was change
The world…now he leads the USA gang.
Today he inspired a lot of people,
And let us know that we are all equal.
Today doesn't seem real, it seems like a dream,
And it really is according to Dr. Martin Luther King.
Today he showed me I can do anything:
President, business owner, maybe even King.
It makes me feel good to have a black President,
Even though my dad's not a real man, Barack is evidence.
Because of him I feel like saying, "Yes, I can,"
To any question asked by any man.
Today Barack gave me lots of hope,
Now I can be "ballin' " without sellin' dope.
Listen to him talk at the inauguration –
Makes me want to read and increase my vocabulation.
Barack makes me feel like "Why settle for less?"
When you can be black and have the best.

Yes, I can. Yes, I can!

THALIA Age 16

Don't Forget Me

I find myself growing up in the system, not in foster care, but in jail, and this makes me feel like I'm getting pushed under layers of dirt down low –

Where people start to forget about me, forget about my problems, forget that I am a human being that makes mistakes.

But no, people forget me and who I am. I'm treated like a criminal, like I don't have needs. What about me? I feel alone in jail.

"Like just another kid" is what they say. Who cares about the family that's affected by me being here?

I find myself slowly slipping away under a stack of folders. And instead of my name on it, it's labeled –

"Just another kid." I'm not just another kid, I'm a kid. And I am not my behavior!

Please don't forget me, who I am.
And please don't remember me
as just another kid.

Dedicated to the world

JUSTIN Age 17

Today

Today I am locked up, in chains, in a cage.

Yesterday I was free, flying, living.

On the street I am running, wanted (!), needed (?).

In my room I am alone, cold, desperate to get out.

To my mom I am sweet, loving, #1 son.

To my dad I am nothing, not known, nobody.

My friends think I am dead, in juvie, lost.

Really I am locked up, alone, a million miles from home...

Dedicated to Momma

SCHOOL YEAR **2007-2008**

The Face of a Cell

JEREMY Age 16

The Face of a Cell

If my cell were a person, it would be a man,
cold and unforgiving.
If he could speak, he would sound like people
talking about what they'll do when they get out.
His face would be ugly, rough and mean.
He would be old with age – a rugged face.
He would just sit there saying in a mean voice,
"You're not going to get out."

Dedicated to the streets

CHAPMAN   Age 17

A Broken Fog

The world is a jungle
The jungle is untamed
There is always a shadow somewhere
Like in Iraq
Where there are enemies running around in the dark
The world's always going to be the same
A hectic place
Wild and unreformed
But changing constantly
Like a struggle for power
Like the way a jungle has an order of life

A jungle
It's exotic
Beautiful
Elegant
Mysterious
Unforgiving

The jungle is a real place
But everything outside is fake
Like the disappearing colors of a rainbow
Imaginary

JESUS Age 14

Gang Pain

I remember the day I got put on.
I fought one-on-one, and we went three rounds,
And the person I was fighting was way older than me.

I was feeling pain everywhere.
The first pain I felt was all over my face,
And that day was a painful day.
And I kept fighting. After all the fighting,
My whole body felt like I was in hell.

I will never forget that day I went through this.
After that I got jumped in it, too, and I think,
Was it worth it?

Dedicated to everybody

How Do I Start a New Beginning

It's hard to start a new beginning
When you've got things holding you back
Being locked up
Probation
No stable housing
Things from when I was a kid
And I can't change what I did
And the system won't let me leave
It feels like they want to keep me here
Like they've got me on a leash
Like I don't have a life
That makes me depressed
It feels like I have to run from myself

JERRY   Age 18

Adult Jail

I turn 18 today.
Today they're going
to take me to jail, adult jail.
Yesterday they told me.

I was mad, so mad that it
made me go to sad. I wanted
to go home. The judge told me
that I can't go home. The prosecuting
attorney said that I am a danger
to society. They always say that.

I have to wait for my trial.
I have two trials: one is the day after
the other. I don't know what
the trial is going to be like. I'm not so
worried about the trial – I think it just
scares me to go to the jail.

I've never been there before,
I don't know what it will be like.
The unknown scares me. People say
different things about the jail – I don't
know who to believe. A crowded cell
filled with mean people who don't
care, returning to prison again and again.

Dedicated to other kids in juvie

MARIUS Age 16

Deep in My Soul

Deep down in my soul
I know that I can change the world
Deep down in my soul
I know I can help people who are living in poverty
Deep down in my soul
I've heard screams
The screams of people who died in my arms

Deep down in my soul
I know I can let people take down the wall
That I have built between myself and society

Deep down in my soul
I know I can learn how to love
Deep down in my soul
I know I can help people help me
Deep down in my soul
I know that the way I learned on the streets is hurtful
Deep down in my soul
I can see myself coming out of poverty

Deep down in my soul
I know that realistically I'm free
But in my soul, I'm not

Deep down in my soul

JON Age 17

Hard to Figure

It's hard to figure out myself

I know that I like to joke around

I don't understand why I can't make my poems rhyme

I know that I like to venture into new things

I don't understand why I can't be the same all the time

I know that I should stop lying

I don't understand why I lie until I believe it

I know that I should be a follower sometimes, rather than always try to be #1

I don't understand why I like to hurt people

I know that I should be the way I used to be

I know that there's a lot of good in me

Dedicated to the ones I love

JAIME Age 14

Race-Blind

He's black, he's white,
Is this what we call races?
I only see mouth, nose, eyes,
Which make up faces.
People call out different colors,
All I see is gray.
We all live here together,
Should it matter anyway?
And who's this guy
I wake up to every day?
Who knows what I see every way
About black and white?
But I don't care
'Cause I only see gray.
The only one that couldn't know me clearer.
Then I realize I'm staring in a mirror.

Dedicated to all kids dealing with racism

TYLER Age 16

Every Native

Every Native grows up just like every other one
To me the definition's pain and suffering
I'm thinking of my tribe
My people are slowly dying
Over alcoholism
We aren't like most Natives with ceremonial rites
We don't even have fishing or travel IDs
We are just fighting for our rights
We don't live on a reservation
We don't have a reservation
You might think we're lucky
But who's really lucky

Every Native grows up like every other one
To me the definition's pain and suffering

I grew up without a Daddy
I was my Mom's only son
Had to put the money on the table
Got a fat burner in my pocket
Cuz drugs was my label
Everybody in my family was unable to quit alcohol
Cuz my family's not stable
You might call us savages
But if you look under our skin
Color and texture down to our skeletons
We all look alike
But to white people, color is all that matters

Every Native grows up like every other one
To me the definition's pain and suffering

PATRICK Age 15

All I Wish

Why act like a whore to express your burning core
You only had four boys and it wasn't enough
You wanted more
Not money or jewelry
But a girl
And no matter how much you prayed
You still didn't notice all the gifts and cards
    you used to discard
It hurt me softly but you hurt me hard
With belts to almost hitting me with your car
Your pepper spray was crucial but your words were brutal
I still hate you and always will
Your gifts and offerings can stand still
All I wish is for love and free will

Dedicated to my brothers

DONALD Age 15

Things That Are Old

Heartbroken by my
father over and over.
Friends bad and good
the way you treat them
reflects back on you over
and over. Reflection
looking at it
over and over.

Feeling sadness, tired,
and left out like they
don't care over and over.
Making new things
in my life, moving on
over and over.

Dedicated to my grandmother

ANTON Age 17

In My Wandering Mind

My brother got taken away from my mom
like a lost child away from home.

Going to trial on two charges
as if they were demons inside
attacking me.

Just the reality of what my sister wrote to me in a letter
like angels answering a lost survivor, gone astray.

Court and release
like freedom waiting to be captured
and brought back to reality.

Like a folded up piece of paper.
Like a shattered mirror
falling slowly in the wind.
Like the black depths beneath the earth
hidden almost like a mask.
Like a blissful angel coming
out in the snow mountains.

I hide my feelings behind a mask
so others can't judge me by my cover.

Dedicated to my family

CALEB   Age 17

Thoughts of a Predicate Felon

I wanna tear down the walls with the rhythm of my
    pounding heart.
I wanna shatter people's thoughts with one parting stare.
I wonder where I'll go.
I know where I wanna be, but I'm having trouble
    getting there.
I try to look at life with a new color: purple, maybe blue.
The colors of the streets are black and gray,
But the color of my thoughts gets lighter by the day.
And though all these new colors are forming around me,
I still feel like a dull pack of crayons without the
    right shade.

Dedicated to A

STEPHEN Age 16

Getting Out in 30 Days

Salt and pepper on my salad,
salt and pepper to wash away
the throw-up, the trouble, things
that aren't mine, the things I wish
I hadn't done. Getting out in 30
days, remembering my mother's
Chicken Adobo, it makes me
smile, it tastes like freedom.

RUBEN Age 16

The River

I'm trapped by society and try to get away,
But can't seem to escape.

But I also see water rushing down the river bank.
Fishes silently still.

My heart races as I enjoy the beautiful view
And sweet scent of water.

There I can be myself
And let out my true emotions,
The love that I hide in a world of violence.
Not feeling scared or having to look behind me.

As I lie here in the grass
Looking up at the sky,
My thoughts are not overclouded.
No sign of locked doors, tiny windows,
Horrible smell.

I'm free.
My heart is a smooth stone
Tumbling to the bottom
Of the river.

Dedicated to myself

AHMED Age 15

My Moment of Birth

I was born,
and the birds were singing.
I was crying. My mom was
holding me in her arms.
I figure my dad was there.
Ambulances were going by.
Pedestrians were roaming
up and down the streets.

Now I am riding my bike, hanging
out with friends. Rocking
side to side, looking around
and wondering where I am.

www.ingramcontent.com/pod-product-compliance
Lightning Source LLC
Chambersburg PA
CBHW050442010526
44118CB00013B/1649